This book is to be returned on or before
the last date stamped below.

LIBREX —

Institute of Latin American Studies
31 Tavistock Square, London WC1H 9HA

9324

British Library Cataloguing-in-Publication Data
A catalogue record for this book is available
from the British Library

ISBN 0 901145 91 2

ISSN 0957-7947

© Institute of Latin American Studies
University of London, 1994

Contents

Walter Belik is a Lecturer in the Institute of Economics, Universidade Estadual de Campinas – UNICAMP, São Paulo, Brazil, and was an Honorary Research Fellow at the Institute of Latin American Studies, University of London, in 1993.

The author wishes to express his thanks for the comments of Fabio Doria Scatolin and for the editing of Margaret Doyle and Oliver Marshall.

The Food Industry in Brazil: Towards a Restructuring?

Introduction

By analysing a country's food consumption patterns it is possible to derive much information on the performance of its food system. The relationship between individuals and food is continuous. Also, the handling of foodstuffs – from purchase to consumption – is routine for most humans. In this way, habits are developed that define a particular cultural pattern for a society.

It is often said that eating is a cultural action, even if only for advertising reasons. In this sense, the circumstances surrounding food purchase and consumption are directly linked to our culture. Moreover, as a dynamic process, the linkage occurs in both directions: we not only consume food according to our culture, but also our culture is shaped by our food habits.

This may be especially true for Brazilian culture. What can be said about a country in which two out of three families are undernourished or live in a chronic state of hunger? In the same way, what can we say about a country which spends US$16.5 billion each year on food consumed outside the home, contributing to a huge fast-food industry? These are some features of Brazilian culture.

Brazil is a country in which urbanisation has progressed rapidly. Nowadays, less than 25% of its population lives in rural areas. Most families, even those at the lowest income level, have a refrigerator, gas cooker and TV. The higher classes own more sophisticated devices, such as microwave ovens and freezers. In other words, the Brazilian consumption pattern is typically urban.

In Brazil, responsibility for the purchase and preparation of food is mostly taken by women. However, with the industrialisation of the economy, more women have joined the labour force and work outside home. At present women comprise almost 50% of the labour force. Nonetheless, women are still expected to provide food for the family's consumption; this is made possible in two alternative or complementary ways: by working extra hours at home or by purchasing more convenience meals. The Brazilian food industry reflects those trends. In fact, it has followed 'step-by-step' those tendencies, even possibly setting the trends itself.

The trajectory of the modern Brazilian food industry began after World War II. Before that, it was possible to observe the presence of industrial capital only in a few sectors in order to complement the food supply to the increasingly urban population. Finally, in the late 1940s and early 1950s, Brazil's food industry boomed. This new phase was based on the diffusion of fordism as a production and consumption paradigm. The modernisation of agriculture and distribution of food products sponsored by governments of the period provided the leverage for this phase.

In the 1980s a new phase of the food industry emerged. New sources of capital arose, new fields of investment appeared and Brazilian companies merged with foreign companies. At the same time, in the developed countries, changes have led to a concentration of suppliers, with increasing participation of the financial sector. Also, on the demand side, market segmentation has been stressed, reflected in the production of more value-added items.

This paper describes the worldwide food industry's new phase – called post-fordist – and its current effects on Brazil. Given the deep changes in the worldwide food industry, what is going to happen in Brazil? Are the great social contrasts and the Brazilian market features compatible with the pattern of modernity that comes from abroad? These are some themes which are analysed in the following sections.

This paper is divided into five sections, followed by a conclusion. Section II describes the origins of the food industry in Brazil. The objective of this analysis is to review the agro-industrial sector formation and capital participation in this process. The third section discusses the performance of agro-industry, chiefly food production, in the context of Brazilian heavy industrialisation in the post-war era. The fourth section presents the latest movements in the Brazilian food system, emphasising the differences between the present sector and its predecessor, which belonged to the first industrialisation boom. The fifth section stresses the main aspects of the restructuring of the food industry in the developed countries. Finally, the conditions in Brazil are assessed in relation to the new configuration of the worldwide food industry.

The Origins of the Brazilian Food Industry

The first agro-processing activity in Brazil was that of the colonial era: molasses and raw sugar exports from sugarcane. After the decline of the colonial sugarcane export boom, this activity was revived after 200 years with the birth of Brazilian industrialisation in the third quarter of the nineteenth century. As will be shown, besides sugar Brazil already had important textile, food and related product industries at the end of the nineteenth century. Thus, the presence of food processing in Brazil is centuries old.

However, a radical change has taken place in food processing in recent decades. The Brazilian agro-industry of the 1970s and 1980s has little in common with that found early in the century. In the past, agro-industry had been an extension of mercantile or agrarian capital.[1] In recent times, these linkages occurred in the reverse way: from financial and industrial capital backwards to agriculture. In other words, the current food industry is not a continuation of that of the last century.

Many authors have worked on the origins of the Brazilian industrialisation process, stressing the dominance of two types of capitalists: importers and coffee producers, which in some cases were the same.[2] The first performed the commercial service, keeping in contact with the main suppliers of capital goods and consumer goods in Europe and the United States. Knowing the market and the main producers, these importers were valuable in supplying proficiency and knowledge to new enterprises. In this almost spontaneous way, an import substitution process took place in the perishable goods sector.

On the other hand, the coffee producers' capital was not only deployed in the coffee plantations, but also in some commercial and industrial businesses. Contrary to common sense, the diversification from coffee was not a strategy of bad years, but a form of expansion in periods of supernormal profits. Prado Jr. (1970, p. 264) shows, for instance, that from 1907, due to government constraints, the expansion of growing areas had ceased and, consequently, a huge amount of capital was relocated into the industrial sector. Given the lack of a structured financial market and the high profits due to coffee's good years, the farmers had exhausted their possibilities of investing in their crops or buying land, railway shares, etc. In this sense the supernormal profits spilled over into industrial activities.

Added to this process was the presence of a class of immigrants. A newly arrived bourgeoisie brought a considerable amount of capital – stocks of commonly imported goods, for example – and settled down as brokers and dealers. Many immigrants could be classified as importers as well, although they had their own peculiarities. Further, these capitalists launched themselves into the industrial domain.

To sum up, the first boom in Brazilian industrialisation, which took place in the last century, could be considered as a diversification based on 'a dynamic of mercantile and financial expansion' (Reiss, 1983, p. 97). The capital of individuals – that of farmers and importers – was linked backwards and forwards. Because of the absence of a mature financial system and few investment opportunities, the same farmers became involved with more advanced production phases, such as processing coffee and other primary products; importers, on the other hand, became involved with earlier production phases by promoting the supply-side.

According to Wilson Cano (1977, p. 129) farmers invested their profits in industry in two ways: directly in factories, and indirectly though banks.[3] Until the third quarter of the nineteenth century, the role of the 'natural economy' was strong in terms of food self-sufficiency on the slave farms. Each farm was an almost autarchic unit; there was no labour division and no monetarisation of contracts. A large number of activities took place inside each farm, such as the production of rustic clothes, tools, carts and even rudimentary machines. Based on Rangel,[4] Paim called this type of organisation the Rural Complex.[5] This phase lasted a long time and was directly related to the level of preferential duties on imported British clothes that inhibited the development of a national industry.

> ... it was best for farmers to redirect their slaves from the innumerable existing farm workshops to rural activities, gradually purchasing in town, at lower prices, products that formerly were produced in these workshops (Paim, 1957, p. 46).[6]

In fact, the development of Brazilian industry was not an expansion of Rural Complex workshop production. Figures produced by research on Brazilian industrialisation show that its national industry had a different origin. In order to supply a rising urban market, competitive with foreign clothing imports, the infant Brazilian textile industry brought machinery from Europe and set up large processing units.

According to Paim, in the 1872 census fewer than two thousand workers were employed in the Brazilian textile factories in towns and cities, compared with four hundred thousand textile workers employed inside farms or small villages (1957, p. 64). The 1907 census registered nearly 52,000 workers in the urban industry; the rural factories no longer had any importance. The progress of the new Brazilian textile industry was remarkable. Dean points out that in the case of the textile industry, 'of the nine cotton mills erected in the 1870s and 1880s, all were sturdily profitable. Still more were built in the city of São Paulo. By 1903, there were thirteen mills employing 2,910 looms' (1969, p. 38).[7]

In most cases, the handicraft industry inside the Rural Complex was stationary, unable to compete with the large apparatus appearing in towns. As has been shown, the origin of this urban manufacturing is related to the commercial capital personified by the farmer, the *comissário* – the coffee dealer – and the coffee growers' bank. In periods of expansion, when the profitability of coffee increased, the coffee capital spilled over towards urban activities supported by the government's protectionist policy.[8]

According to Prado Jr. (1970, p. 261) World War I gave a great boost to these industrial activities. A depreciated exchange rate not only blocked the imports of many industrial goods, but also allowed Brazil to export to a huge international market which was under-supplied due to the war.

A new wave of investments also arose at the end of World War I based on a spell of good years for coffee. Suzigan has pointed out that 'the cotton oilseed industry received new investment in 1920-21 when seven oil factories and one central factory and refinery were established by only one company' (1986, p. 87). Moreover, the early Brazilian meat processors, the first cement factory and other new enterprises were direct results of the coffee valorisation programme, while a fragile monetary expansion occurred in 1922-23. The overall effect of these policies was a remarkable appreciation of the exchange rate and, combined with the trade difficulties imposed by the war, they were the main causes of the birth of such important industries as paper and shoes, led by traditional importers.

From 1929, in the period of deep economic crisis, coffee capital was released from the new capitalist ventures, becoming fully independent. Purchasing cheap, secondhand equipment from abroad, factory owners were able to expand far beyond the limits of their original coffee capital. According to Cardoso de Mello, the consumer goods industry, which emerged as the single largest industry, came about because 'the technology was relatively elementary, easy to handle and self-contained in the equipment available in the international market. Also the plant size and the initial investment were easily suitable to the Brazilian economy of that time' (1975, p. 162). As a result of all these factors, in fewer than twenty years Brazil began production in roughly all sectors of light industry, as well as in some intermediate and capital goods, such as the railway supplies industry.

The primary characteristic of Brazilian agro-industry at the beginning of this century was its mercantile basis. Indeed, until World War I the main source of capital invested in industry was the indigenous commercial capital, given that foreign investment was almost nonexistent and there was little reinvestment of profits from industrial capital.[9] The agro-industry that was revived in the 1950s, however, and which accompanied a new and consolidated durable goods sector and a new urban society, was not simply a continuation of the previous agro-industry. The intensive and extensive import substitution process, which began in the 1930s, and the heavy industrialisation of the 1950s, contributed greatly to a new configuration of the old industry.

According to Tavares (1977, p. 76), between 1929 and 1938, imports of consumer goods fell 70%. This led to an import substitution process in elementary goods – food, drink and other consumables – that, given the level of urbanisation, was stimulated by market dynamism.[10] Padis (1977, p.238) writes: 'The 1929 crisis, having promoted a general decrease in prices, led to a fall in the import capacity of traditional Latin American countries'.[11]

From the 1930s crisis until 1948, the import substitution policy developed smoothly. The process worked on many levels, but in different ways.

> (In Brazil) it was almost impossible to have an industrialisation process that moved smoothly from the base to the top of the production pyramid – that is, starting with less elaborate consumer goods and going, slowly, until it reached capital goods (Tavares, 1977, p. 46).[12]

Here, the modernisation of traditional sectors and the subsequent import substitution could not take place without forcing the emergence of capital goods, intermediate and durable goods. These bottlenecks were obstacles to sustainable and endogenous economic growth.

The modernisation of light industries such as food, textiles and pulp and paper required a wider and firmer basis. The account given by Pires and Bielschowsky (1978) of the dairy industry of the 1940s reflects the period's agro-industrial conditions. Milk processing and its market expansion were blocked due to the lack of basic equipment. Some equipment such as pasteurisers, tanks and creamers were produced in Brazil only in the 1950s; others, such as powdered milk and cheese-making equipment, only in the 1960s.

The broadening of industry was taking place at the same time that agriculture took a new form. In fact, from the 1940s agriculture and agro-industry accompanied the growth of further industrial sectors. There is no evidence that these primary-based industrial sectors spurred the growth of the other sectors; on the contrary, agro-industry in general was directly dependent on imported machines, equipment and inputs supplies. Agriculture's dependence on such equipment was particulary strong given the standards and regularity of raw materials required (see Kageyama, 1990, p. 48).

With the new linkages between agriculture and industry developing in the 1950s and 1960s, industry started to create new products, which were much more uniform and were produced in a regular flow. A new articulation of agriculture and industry, very different from that known earlier in the century, began to develop.

At first, articulation moved forward, from agriculture to industry, through a vertical integration of agrarian and mercantile capital. The 1960s saw a distinct change. Industrial sources of capital, many of them transnational and taking advantage of the federal government's policy, were established in the consumer goods sector. From this base, the new capital pursued links with agriculture, selling capital goods for agriculture and other inputs. In contrast to the generally anarchic nature of capitalism, the Brazilian state pointed the way, which industry then followed.

In conclusion, it is important to underline that these early industries were distinct from modern agro-industry. The reasons for early industry's failure to gain a foothold are diverse and require a wide analysis of both the Brazilian and the worldwide economy at the turn of the century (see Cardoso de Mello, 1975). Here it is enough to say that from this first industrial boom based on non-durable goods, processing activities underwent slow changes. However, the durable and capital goods sectors changed quickly, reaching an almost complete form of industrial economy in the 1950s and 1960s.

The leading factor in this new articulation of agriculture and industry was the involvement of the state through its management and public policies instituted in the 1960s. From that point, the links between agriculture and industry relied on regulation by the government and major sectorial interest groups.

Growth Without Deepening

At the end of World War II new market opportunities opened for US industry in Europe. US companies expanded their overseas capital investments by entering countries that had been devastated by the war. Opportunities were seen in both directions: traditional European firms started to see in Latin America an area sheltered from the US commercial advance. This movement led to the establishment in Brazil – in the late 1940s and 1950s – of many divisions of European companies which, together with United States firms, introduced in Brazil the modern processed food industry.[13]

> This new and more advanced form taken by the internationalisation of capital – the financial conglomerate – was manifested through the penetration of US companies in Canada, the United Kingdom and continental Europe taking advantage of post-war reconstruction programmes. Their considerable financial advantages menaced the stability of European companies that were forced to accept this challenge by moving to a new territory that would, perhaps, be more favourable. One could explain in this way the export of European capital [to Brazil] and the relative disinterest of US large companies, which were much more interested in the solid and promising European markets, where their participation had been relatively small (Cardoso de Mello, 1975, p. 127).

According to Candal (1977, p. 245), Brazilian industrialisation did not occur in the classic form of intensified mass consumption, as it did in Europe. The first phase of Brazilian industrialisation – based on traditional goods consumption – remained stable for a long period. At the same time, industry was not diversified until the 1920s due to the erratic and selective policy on imports.

The 1930s crisis followed by World War II and the intensive process of capital internationalisation led to an expansion of Brazilian industry. Not surprisingly, agro-industry had lost ground to other industrial sectors. The textile and food segments contributed more than 50% of the industrial gross product during the first half of the twentieth century (Tavares, 1977, p.92). Nevertheless, from the end of World War II heavy foreign and state investments in sectors producing durable goods led to increasing diversification of industry, reducing the importance of the textile and food industries.

A limited comparison using official data from the first half of this century reveals that in relative terms agro-industry lost ground to other industrial sectors. According to Muller (1981, p. 47): '... it has been stated that the agroindustrial sectors reached a participation ceiling in the 1950s, which subsequently declined'. Indeed, an analysis of the 1985 industrial census data shows that the agro-industry share in the total industrial product remained at the level of 24.5% (see table I).[14] However, internally there were many changes in the agro-industry. A new economic structure arose in the early 1960s, with oligopolistic forms emerging in agro-industry. At the same time, foreign capital infiltrated some hegemonic areas belonging to national companies.

Table I
Brazil: Share of Agro-Industry in Total Industry (1960-1985) (%)

	1960	1970	1980	1985
Number of establishments	33.4	30.5	32.7	35.7
Number of workers	21.1	19.8	21.5	29.7
Value added	30.8	25.4	24.4	24.5

Sources: Muller (1981, p. 46) and FIBGE (1990)

A comparison of the capital composition of all agro-industrial sectors in recent decades with the composition of this capital in the import substitution phase reveals important changes. The old agro-industrial capital was completely replaced by a new capital – national or foreign – having a new competitive pattern, based on oligopolist practices.

The post-war years might be characterised by the abundance of new sources of capital that started to operate in new areas of food industry. This new expansion cycle had the following features:

i) The spread of US consumption patterns based on canned food and semi-processed meals.
The great marketing effort to introduce new consumption habits was well rewarded by the diffusion of the so-called 'US way of life'. The penetration of advertising through new media channels was instrumental to the success of this US 'raid'.

ii) The dissemination of new food retailing equipment relying on self-service procedures.
The first supermarket, Supermarket Sirva-se or 'help yourself', was established in São Paulo in 1953 by foreign tobacco group Souza Cruz.[15] In the same year, in the industrial town of São José dos Campos, another supermarket was opened, managed by one of the biggest textile companies – Tecelagem Paraíba. In the former Brazilian capital, Rio de Janeiro, the first supermarkets were established in 1955; one of them – SU-CO Supermarket – benefited from US expertise. After ten years, Brazil's supermarkets had more than 1,000 points-of-sale.

Today the supermarket business is the main activity of Brazil's commercial sector. According to *Superhiper* magazine – the official publication of the supermarket owners' association – in 1989 the industry had a turnover of 4.6% of Brazilian GNP and employed 538,000 people in 33,801 shops. The industry is also responsible for 80% of food supplies in Brazil.[16] Figures from the last Brazilian economic census – 1985 – show that supermarkets and hypermarkets distributed 78% of the packed meat, 74% of fresh fruits and vegetables, 72% of grains and 71% of dairy goods, among others.[17]

iii) Government support for new food industries and foreign capital investment.
In this period a complete change occurred in the sector's capital structure, which became increasingly oligopolistic. Roger Burbach and Patricia Flynn (1982), in their research on the entrance of US capital in the Latin American food industry, point to the establishment in Brazil of the following transnational companies in the post-war years: Anderson Clayton (oil refineries, 1948), Carnation (Leite Gloria, 1960), Coca-Cola (instant coffee, 1957), CPC International (Dextrina, 1963), Del Monte Corp. (canned fruits and vegetables, n.d.), General Foods Corp. (Kibon, 1957), Kellogg Co. (cereals, 1962), King Ranch Inc. (meats, 1954), Pepsi Co. (soft drinks, 1951), Quaker Oats (oats,

1954), Standard Brands (starch, coffee and milk, 1957) and Warner Lambert (confectionery, 1962) among others.

Moreover, new European investments in the period can be added to this list. Some traditional European companies opened branches or reinforced their investments in Brazil. Also, a new nucleus of Brazilian companies was formed in the food industry. The main segment of Brazilian capital investment was in flour mills, pasta, canned conserves, sauces and dairy products.

The following three case studies in the Brazilian food industry are useful in comparing the origins and structure of capital from the first phase to the second phase. Some industrial enterprises in the early twentieth century had in their further development clear examples of all the above mentioned transformations.

Slaughterhouses

The early slaughterhouses were established in Brazil in the late nineteenth century. They were modest and aimed to supply the growing urban demand. The large slaughterhouses arose only in the 1910s in the states of São Paulo, Rio de Janeiro and Minas Gerais, not only to supply internal demand, but also to export to struggling countries in Europe.

The advent of large firms in this sector had begun with the arrival in 1913 of Wilson – one of the biggest groups in meat processing in the United States (see Suzigan, 1986, p. 335). In addition, the British Anglo company arrived in 1912; in 1917 the Brazilian Meat Company entered the industry and later the US companies Armour (1917) and Swift (1919) became involved. Enterprises belonging to the Matarazzo family and those of national groups also participated in this period.

These companies, which survived for more than fifty years, rapidly declined in the 1960s. At this time they were being replaced by new national groups such as Bordon, Mouran, La Villete, Kaiowa and by others who came from poultry processing such as Sadia, Perdigão, Chapecó, Frangosul, Seara (Hering). In fact, almost all companies that initiated their activities in this industry in the early part of the century were sold or closed down, with their assets being incorporated into new groups.[18]

The turning point in this sector might be observed at the beginning of the 1960s, when most of the foreign companies were not flexible enough to adjust to the rapid market changes. The national groups, favoured by the increasingly strict sanitation regulations and enjoying state support and access to scarce sources of raw materials, became leaders in the industry.

Sugarcane Industry
The modern nucleus of the sugar agro-industry was established in the 1920s in São Paulo (Cano, 1977, p. 67; Szmerecsányi, 1986, p. 29). Some activity in sugar production and refining already existed in the late nineteenth century, but the great impulse was given by the coffee crisis when millions of 'rubiaceae' trees were eradicated. The former 'sugar square' constituted by Sorocaba, Piracicaba, Jundiaí and Mogi Guaçu[19] was enlarged, and the state of São Paulo abandoned its main role of refiner, having only a small share of supply,[20] and became a large sugarcane producer.

In the 1930s new sugarmills were erected in Sertãozinho, Cravinhos, Araraquara, Pontal and other towns of the interior of São Paulo. According to Ramos (1983) the four biggest sugar companies of this period, whose combined share was 64.2% of the national sugar product between 1930-31 and 1935-36, were: Société des Sucreries Brasiliennes (28.2%), Morganti (17.3%), Francisco Junqueira (9.8%) and Matarazzo (8.9%). From the late 1940s onwards the Central-Southern region surpassed the traditional Northeast as a whole, and São Paulo was consolidated as the dynamic heart of the sugar agro-industry.

At the same time as marriages and fusions among traditional sugar clans continued, a radical change occurred in the *'paulista'*[21] sugar framework over a thirty-year period. In the 1940s new groups were established;[22] these were derived from industry – Biagi, Dedini Brothers and Zillo-Lorenzetti, for example; from the financial sector – such as Silva Gordo (Banco Português); and also from building works such as the Balbos.[23]

Due to the sugar expansion in the 1970s and later, in 1975, the birth of the Pro-alcohol Program, a new wave of capital entered the industry, and from this period onwards the industry had a new capital structure. Some names from the 1940s and 1950s flourished, including Ometto, Dedini, Biagi and Zanini. Even though a few sugar businesses from early in the century remained – such as Matarazzo or Junqueira – their importance was reduced. Also the *'usineiros'*[24] from the Northeast, the powerful latifundio class that ruled local politics, lost importance, giving way to *'paulistas'*.

In the late 1970s a new dimension emerged in this sector. The most modern and powerful productive capital was found in two consortia: the COPERSUCAR – Central Cooperative of Sugar and Alcohol Producers – and the SOPRAL – Sugar and Alcohol Producers' Society. Their members were the new capitalist corporations, cooperatives, traditional groups and other businesses related to the sugarcane industry.

From the 1980s onwards the largest sugarcane mills – in terms of sugarcane milling volume – were all part of this new generation.[25] None among the big sugarmills and autonomous alcohol distilleries belonged to the old generation. COPERSUCAR, which comprises 70 sugarmills and five autonomous distilleries in the centre-south region, in 1990-91 reached a share of 27.9% of total Brazilian sugarcane output, 26.7% in sugar and 30.3% in alcohol. Moreover, the COPERSUCAR group also operates in coffee and other food products, making it the biggest Brazilian food company.[26]

These changes experienced in the centre-south dynamic nucleus of the sugarcane agro-industry did not occur at the same pace in the northeast. There, a movement of centralisation leading to mergers took place in the inter-war period. Later, in the pro-alcohol phase, new groups and groups derived from traditional corporations turned to ethanol production on a modern basis, mainly in the state of Alagoas. Nevertheless, considering the capital structure of the groups involved in the process, no major change occurred in the northeast.[27]

Flour-Milling Industry
Capital that participates in the flour-milling industry in Brazil has its origins in the first industrialisation boom of the late nineteenth century. Grain and wheatflour importers, with warehouses located in the main ports, started to widen their activities by setting up flour mills. Although many mergers occurred at that time, the foreign and the traditional local companies remained.

The case of flour mills might be presented as an exception to the generally rapidly changing food industry. Nonetheless, two important new elements contributed to making this case an exception: the ruin of the old colonial mills in the south and premature state intervention.

State intervention establishing ceilings on price and quantity controls began in the 1920s. With this policy the government succeeded in removing from the market the small competitors, who were integrated in agricultural production. From that time the sector was increasingly concentrated in a few large mills (Muller, 1980). However, the colonial mills – established to process wheat for domestic and regional demand in the southern states of Brazil – survived until the late 1970s.

Suzigan (1986) explains that four groups controlled almost all wheat flour production in Brazil in the 1920s: the British Rio Flour Mills, the Argentine Bunge & Born, and Matarazzo and Moinho Fluminense, both Brazilian. These four groups together had an internal system that allowed them to establish quotas while at the same time obstructing the entry of new competitors. Based on this system, these companies succeeded in expanding the milling capacity of the northeast using preferential imports of wheat from the United States.

Later on, in the 1950s, due to the cheap wheat policy and the incentives given to consumers, the industry progressed rapidly. The quota system only benefited the established firms, those big companies approving the cartel's supply management. There was no room for the new investors, which led the entrepreneurs towards related areas in downstream activities. From the 1950s onwards many companies were installed in the pasta, biscuits, bread and other segments of the food industry without any possibility of backward integration due to the quota system.

Trying to end the ongoing food crisis in the early 1960s, the military government imposed a state monopoly on wheat in 1967. The government bought up wheat – from Brazilian farmers and abroad – in order to sell it to mills. The wheat prices as well as the flour produced were officially controlled, with the government managing the prices and subsidies to indigenous farmers and mills in order to stabilise the supply.

When this system ended in 1990, because of the government's commitment to reducing its expenses, the sector's production was one third of its processing capacity. As the flour mills were not allowed to increase their output over their quotas, and the prices were controlled, there was no competition among companies. In that sense the only way to discourage new entries was through increasing capacity.

These distortions made the wheat-flour mills one of the most concentrated economic sectors in Brazil. Bunge & Born had 30% of the quotas in the late 1980s. The profits came from the 5% sales margin guaranteed by government, and mostly from the differences between sales and purchasing terms.

After deregulation, the flour mill industry began changing quickly. Many trading companies are now investing in this activity, replacing government in supplying wheat and seeking integration forward. As a consequence, prices are falling rapidly and traditional companies are near collapse. On the other hand, new sources of capital have entered this saturated sector as independent companies or as a result of backward integration.

The Trajectory of the Food Industry in Brazil

Although the cases of meat processors, sugar mills and the milling industry have been discussed, it is necessary to put all these examples in the food industry into context. Until now, two phases can be seen in the development of the food industry in Brazil. The observations on the performance of the Brazilian food industry contained in this section illustrate the emergence of a third phase in which industrial restructuring is the main subject.

The two phases seen up to this point are as follows:

The initial phase corresponds to the first industrialisation boom from the last quarter of the nineteenth century. In this phase the presence of flour mills, animal fats and oil factories, slaughterhouses and sugar refineries brought together a circle of small and medium-sized companies[28] facing an increasingly urban population.

Most of the capital goods used by the food industry were imported, and the economic dynamism came from abroad. The performance of coffee determined the industry's rate of expansion, due to its dependence on employment and urbanisation.

The second phase, initiated in the post-war period, placed the food sector in a broader industrialisation context. In this phase, new capital – from both national and foreign sources – developed additional areas for investment and also rejuvenated the trajectory of the old food industry.

A different market environment then arose with new consumer habits. The emergence of supermarkets and convenience foods radically transformed the suppliers developing the fordist paradigm all over the world. In Brazil, these effects started to be felt in the late 1950s. However, because of the characteristics of the Brazilian market, the fordist model of consumption and production did not take root.

In the late 1970s, the Brazilian food industry entered its *third phase*. This new phase can be attributed to the emergence of new competitors and new sources of capital in the industry. As occurred in the former two phases, a new capital wave flooded the food sector, re-establishing links with other segments of the food system. Two events contributed to the development of this new phase.

On the one hand, the beginning of industrial economic restructuring in the developed world (see Tavares, 1992) led to new forms of competition, as companies reviewed their overseas strategies. Also contributing to this new phase were rising economic protectionism, the 1980s recession in the developed world, and the emergence of trade blocs.

On the other hand, the long economic recession, the collapse of state industrial intervention, and substantial changes occurring within and among firms all contributed to a new environment, displacing the state as a regulator of industrial development and opening new fields for investment.

As a result of these two factors, foreign investment in the Brazilian food industry increased and represented the main field of interest for foreign capital in the period 1969-90.[29] However, it is not only foreign capital that increased its investments in food industries; many Brazilian companies merged with competitors and entered new fields and new markets. The presence of Brazilian banks and other conglomerates in the production field, especially in agro-industry, is one striking feature of this.

Table II lists the main partnerships or mergers in this third phase of the food industry in Brazil, using available data from the period 1985-91. This is only a small sample of the changes occurring in publicly quoted companies or companies for which public announcements were made. Table II does not include investments made by established firms in their own companies.

The changes experienced by the Brazilian food industry in 1985-91, as shown in Table II, represent a radical change in most segments of industry. In addition to the listed acquisitions and mergers, many Brazilian and foreign groups entered new or stable product groups such as orange juice, vegetable oils, animal feed, dehydrated food, wines and beverages.

Table II
Brazil: Partnerships, Joint Ventures or Mergers in the Food Industry (1985-91)

New Entries	Origin	Acquired Company	Product Group
Dart & Kraft	USA	Embaré	Confectionery
Nestlé	SWI	Ailiram[1] e Buitoni	Pasta
Bunge & Born	ARG	Petybon	Pasta
Nabisco	USA	Jupiter	Pasta
Pepsi Co	USA	Elma Chips	Pasta
Borden	USA	Adria e Romanini	Pasta
Quaker Oats	USA	Toddy e Coqueiro	Choc/Fish
Philip Morris	USA	Kibon, Sorvane, Lacta[2] e Q'Refresco[3]	Ice Cream Choc/Beverages
Hershey Foods	USA	Petybon[4] e Lacta	Pasta/Choc
Fleishmann Royal	USA	Maguary[5]	Ice Cream/Juice
Ferruzzi Spa	ITA	Cica	Preserves
M. Mars	USA	Neugebauer	Chocolate
Danone Gervais	FRA	Chandler e LPC	Dairy/Choc

New Entries	Origin	Acquired Company	Product Group
Parmalat	ITA	Teixeira, Supremo Via Lacta e Alimba[6]	Dairy
Bongrain (Polenghi)	FRA	Scandia, C.Limpo[7]	Dairy
MD Foods	DEN	Vigor	Dairy
Gessy Lever	GB/HOL	Queijos Rex e Luna	Dairy
Sodima	FRA	Lacesa (Yoplait)	Dairy
Mansur (Leco)	BRA	Flôr da Nata	Dairy
CPC (Ref. Milho Bras)	USA	McCormick e Kitano	Sauces
Sadia	BRA	Frig. Mouran	Meat
Perdigão	BRA	Chapecó[8], Sulina e Borella	Meat
Hering (Ceval)	BRA	La Villete e Betinha	Meat
Bordon	BRA	Swift-Armour	Meat

Notes:
[1] Belonged to Beatrice Foods (USA)
[2] Lacta had been acquired by Suchard (FRA) and Philip Morris controlled 40% of the shares
[3] Philip Morris owned 45% of the shares
[4] Joint venture with Santista (Bunge & Born - ARG). The company also has a joint venture with LPC-Danone (FRA)
[5] Belonged to Souza Cruz (USA)
[6] Also Laticínios Alpha and S. Helena, less important acquisitions
[7] Also Laticínios Aujuroca and Santa Rosa
[8] Perdigão owned 43% of shares

The table lists partnerships of foreign companies followed by those of national companies. ARG: Argentina; BRA: Brazil; DEN: Denmark; USA: United States of America; FRA: France; GB: Great Britain; HOL: Holland; ITA: Italy; SWI: Switzerland.

Source: Research in specialised press

The Table suggests a new investment wave which, as has been pointed out before, represents a new trajectory similar to that occurring in the developed countries. Data from the Brazilian Central Bank confirm that in the last decade US$2.5 billion of foreign capital was invested in agro-industry, of which more than US$1 billion was destined for the food industry.

In a world framework, these Brazilian movements coincide with a wider change in positions involving the main international food production and distribution companies. According to Pérez and Oncuoglu (1990), these movements in the international food industry are called 'structural operations' due to their ability to change the sector's morphology. These movements are also related to a new form of competition. Huge mergers and transactions set this phase in an international framework.[30] However, even more dramatic than changing assets is the substantial transformation of the competitive environment.

In regard to capital positioning, there is no doubt that the Brazilian food industry is entering a new phase. Many aspects must be examined, however, to confirm this trend. As in the international framework, a restructuring process is based on more elements than a simple shift in the ownership of assets. These elements will be investigated in detail in the next sections of this paper, which constitute the central subject of the author's research.

A New Paradigm in the Food Industry of Developed Countries

Unlike many other goods, food maintains a constant and recurring relationship with consumers. Decisions on what and how to consume food are taken every moment. Product attributes such as quality and price are constantly evaluated by consumers. Also, the final food production is distinct from other types of production due to its basic regional characteristics. Massive exports of prepared food are not common in any developed or developing country and are considered to be 'market deformities'.

During the post-war period, many factors contributed to the emergence of a pattern of so-called fordist consumption. Among these factors are the following:

i) The food shortage in Europe and the aid and recovery programmes led by the USA.[31] The great production effort in agriculture and industry permitted, in global terms, the transition from a food deficit and hunger to overproduction in fifteen years.

ii) High price elasticity of food products. Given the economic depression in Europe and other regions, growth in demand was directly related to increases in household income and product price reduction.

iii) The effective penetration of media and advertising and the homogenisation of habits and demand. This occurred with the introduction of television when mass communication became a reality.

iv) Generalisation of oligopolistic behaviour in the food industry. The first oligopolies in the food sector were established (mostly in the United States) early in the 1920s. In the post-war period the presence of huge corporations intensified, in spite of the implementation of thorough anti-monopoly legislation in the USA and Europe. The United Kingdom, for instance, passed restrictive legislation that considered some activities, such as the food industry, to be in the 'public interest'.

v) The gradual rise in the scale of production. The optimal scale of production increased because of the generalisation of consumption on the one hand and, on the other, the desire to impose barriers to entry by existing suppliers.

vi) The low participation of larger units in the food distribution sector. Until the early 1950s, food retailing was based on small business, well dispersed and very specialised. At this time, retailing had not experienced the self-service revolution.

All these factors set the conditions for the introduction of a new competitive, fordist, pattern within the international food industry. The fordist accumulation pattern aims for mass production and falling costs in order to supply uniform products for mass consumption.

The participation of transnational companies in many segments of the food industry can be linked to their strategy to supply markets through mass production, low prices and margins in the post-war period. Enormous business structures were constructed to support the expansion of the international companies into new markets, offering homogeneous food products to compete with local companies, local tastes and local consumer habits. The predominance of transnational companies was established all over the world through their brands, prices and revolutionary way of marketing.

Berhman (1984), analysing the competitive strategy of international food companies, describes them as 'market seekers' due to the constant need to widen their consumption and production bases. Investigating the food firms, Rama (1992a) underlines the fact that the competition in this field is from country to country, contributing to the multidomestic characteristic of the food industry. This is in contrast to most international industry, in which competition is global.

Given this competitive pattern, the management of these companies is required to have widespread knowledge of the market. Issues such as brand fidelity and constant consumption are everyday concerns for international companies in each country. Advertising and cultural environment have been the most important weapons in the food supply competition. Nonetheless, without low prices the goal of mass consumption would never be reached. In this sense, the expansion of the food industry in the post-war period can only be explained by the constitution of a 'virtuous circle' of growth.

In this period, flourishing consumption was provided for by the addition of new production units with huge advertising investments. Increasing agricultural output and the standardisation of raw materials, given the new crop techniques, allowed low costs and cheap prices to filter down to the consumer. And finally, continuous employment growth supplied the market with new waves of consumers eager to spend their earnings. All these elements converged to form a 'virtuous circle' of capital accumulation.

The continuous enlargement of this circle allowed an enormous supply to be concentrated in the hands of a few companies which held a considerable market share. In the late 1980s, the ten largest firms in the world agro-food sector had a turnover of US$185 billion in production and trade activities (Rastoin and Allaya, 1990). As an additional basis of comparison, according to the International Labour Organisation the food industry was the largest industry in the world, with a turnover of US$800 billion in 1975 (ILO, 1984). In spite of the different dates and sources, these figures show that the power of big companies is striking.[32]

According to Williamson (1985), the oligopolistic predominance in particular activities cannot be explained by the traditional theory of barriers. On the contrary, the output concentration generally is linked to a successful strategy to reduce transaction costs. The main feature of this strategy is vertical integration. Vertical integration leads to more output concentration, which seldom translates into reduction of final prices.

This is exactly the case of the food industry. The main objective of integration in this industry has always been to lower the costs of suppliers. Such integration should lead to falling prices. Nevertheless, what takes place is exactly the contrary: evidence shows that processed food prices are rising in spite of a drop in costs of agricultural raw materials.[33]

Data from 1977 for the United States show that three-quarters of output in the food industry has come from structures considered to be oligopolies. Integration contracts are the most conventional structural form of production. In the United States, for instance, integration contracts are responsible for more than 90% of the supply in some segments such as poultry, milk, sugarbeet etc. (Marion, 1985). In Europe, the situation is the same. Many European companies are being prosecuted by government agencies under anti-trust legislation in areas such as sugar, tinned vegetables and baby-foods, among others (Maunder, 1983).

Given the market saturation experienced from the early 1970s and the impossibility of further large productivity gains, the fordist strategy of accumulation reveals some problems. In short, the fordist production and consumption pattern has fallen into crisis.

On the one hand, due to the particular shape of the demand curve and given household income, the demand for food is relatively inelastic. Consumers are spending proportionally less than ever on food. In the developed countries spending on food has not followed the population's rise in income. Also, with the world recession in the last few years, consumers have spent less and purchase only the essentials. In the United Kingdom, food spending in the home and outside the home fell from 29% of household income in the 1960s to 17.2% in the 1980s, and then to 12.7% in the early 1990s (Burns, 1983; Goodman and Redclift, 1990; IMF, 1993).[34] In Italy this proportion was 20% (Fanfani and Montresor, 1991) and in the USA only 17% in the 1980s (Ritson et al, 1986).

The food industry is representative of the well-known Engel's Law, given family size and dietary habits. As food consumption has shrunk as a proportion of income, industry's only alternative in order to increase profits on sales to the highest levels of household income is by adding value to their products.

The food consumption crisis is the other side of the agricultural crisis (Goodman and Redclift, 1990). The agricultural growth that followed the post-war period was tuned to a fordist diet. Mass marketing, advertising and standard products were the characteristics of this phase. To quote Goodman and Redclift (1990, p. 20), 'It is at the level of food manufacturing and consumption, rather than agricultural production, that the analogy with "fordism" in this industry is most apposite....' Given the market saturation, the fordist diet entered a crisis requiring a gradual restructuring of industry and market strategies.

Two of the main social elements that have provided the impulse to the new fordist pattern in the post-war period are presenting continuing problems: the expansion of female labour and the increasing variety and use of labour-saving home appliances. First, the women going out to work opened the way for new, more practical and convenient food products. Secondly, the housewife began to rely on additional appliances, transferring the traditional hard work of preparing and cooking ingredients to the factory environment. With the proper appliances and convenience foods, tasks in the kitchen were reduced.

Common sense suggests that the introduction of ready-to-cook food and new appliances freed women from housework giving them opportunities in the labour market. However, as Goodman and Redclift (1991) point out, the direction of this causality is exactly the opposite. Women were compelled to work outside the home and contribute to the family budget, and the food industry responded by providing the necessary support to facilitate housework tasks. The food industry had to begin offering more practical meals, and the retail sector had to exhibit new and more convenient formats of sale. Finally, a new, important segment arose in the food industry: the profitable catering service.[35]

Nonetheless, from the mid-1970s these two expansionary elements of demand collapsed. Female participation in the labour market reached its ceiling of 50% in most developed countries. Also, the demand for new home appliances was reduced; most kitchens now have all the gadgets they can sustain. From this environment, the implementation of new strategies regarding the growth of production became much more intense. The main source of growth was not the horizontal widening of consumption, but its deepening through product differentiation.

The outstanding growth of profit margins reached by companies illustrated this new phase of industry. In spite of the so-called 'consumer crisis', the profitability of the remaining industry post-concentration, as well as the added value provided, increased in the 1980s. According to Rama (1992a, p. 58), between the 1960s and the 1980s profits after taxes in the US food industry grew from 7% to 10% of sales.[36] In the United States, for instance, the food sector is the leader among industry's nineteen sectors. This sector – including tobacco and beverages – in 1980 contributed 14% of the entire US value added (Connor et al, 1985).

The food industry expands slowly in developed countries; its growth rate is less than the rate of population growth.[37] Nevertheless, the competitive strategy of international food companies is adjusted to supply goods to this saturated market. Given their enormous population growth and also economic growth, one would expect developing countries to be the main investment field for transnational food companies. However, in general these companies prefer to invest in saturated markets in developed countries. An overview of investments on the part of the US food industry has shown that developing countries represented only around 23% of investment destinations in the last decade; Europe had roughly two-thirds of total investment (Rama, 1992a).

This new transnational positioning can no longer be considered typically fordist. The competition is not measured now by market size but by intensity of consumption, particularly in terms of increasing the value added of products. The First World consumer will always be motivated to consume since the products available fulfil the requirements of convenience, taste, appearance and quantity. The consumer will be eager to spend what is necessary in order to satisfy these requirements.

The former fordist companies were forced to change to face a global demand, making large investments in marketing to overcome differentiations by social class and region. Such transformations have led to a new competitive pattern in the past two decades. This new environment has caused the mainstream theoretical framework to be re-examined. Indeed, the cost theoretical transaction model does not suit the new production conditions. Considering the agro-food system as a whole, the problem is not only to reduce transaction costs, but also to regain *flexibility* and *quality*.

According to the original theory, transaction costs are a necessary part of shifts in the productive system. Transaction costs are different from other costs of production, which are the basis of neoclassical theory. Williamson (1985) stated that transaction costs are the equivalent of friction in physics.

The absence of friction in any natural system is unrealistic. The same is true for an economic system. Transactions costs can explain why certain competitive structures were erected. In other words, transaction costs theory helps explain how economic agents behave in the search for reducing friction. Verticalisation is one of many strategies of cost reduction. Franchising, joint ventures and distribution agreements are further forms of the relationship between agents. However, all these related forms have the same characteristic: they are relatively stable and assume collaboration schemes between the agents.

Changes in supply orientation are transforming mass production into a differentiated and segmented production. The collaboration between agents tends to be extended and more permanent. The relationship between firms is no longer guided by market mechanisms. Issues such as price, quality and delivery terms are discussed in parallel agreements. This might be said to be a new stage, given the collaboration between agents and having 'a new paradigm based on solidarity between actors who work together in the same production wisdom that flows from demand to supply' (Green and Rocha dos Santos, 1992a, p. 209). This new solidarity paradigm is called the network economy.

Using the example of Toyota's integration model, Williamson (1985) underlines that this company and its suppliers worldwide have a common development project. Despite common interests, the contract renovation between Toyota and its suppliers is not automatic. The Japanese company uses its power to promote competition among its suppliers and this has a frictional cost. The network economy model allows for such arrangements, making it unlikely that friction will be totally eliminated between agents.

As has been noted, another relevant difference between the network economy and the traditional model is that in the network the main concern is to improve the process as a whole. In improving the efficiency, the origin of the inputs – the company's own inputs or those of external suppliers – matters less than the optimisation of 'the entire cost from different actors related to productive operation, and useless questioning of who is the capital's owner' (Green and Rocha dos Santos, 1992a, p. 208).

The network economy paradigm holds a post-fordist rationale that touches directly on the performance of the agrofood system today. The changes in the agro-food system, due to consumer sophistication and low price elasticity, led to new forms of production without addressing the issues of cost reduction and scales of production. Nowadays, consumers' decisions are based on a thorough consideration of their needs. Consumers participate in a large number of food-related transactions every day. Enjoying high income and choice, consumers will spontaneously adopt a differentiated diet. In this context, the fordist diet loses out to alternatives like 'healthy foods', 'ethnic foods', and others.

These changes on the demand side affect the entire food chain, making a flexible adjustment in the production process. This shift occurs mainly in the following operations:

    1. Food production procedures
    2. The capital-labour relationship
    3. Product circulation
    4. The inter-companies relationship.

The effect of these changes in agriculture is widespread. In this sector the adjustment is prolonged and difficult, given that most innovation is outside agriculture. It has not yet been possible to customise agricultural products for commercial purposes. It is quite difficult producing animal or vegetable goods on a large scale for each market segment in a short period. Until now, agriculture has had marginal participation in the post-fordist dynamic. In general, product customisation takes place in the industrial environment by means of bleaching and adding flavourings, regulators and artificial preservatives. Although there are forms of product customisation in the agricultural field, most of these processes do considerable damage to the environment.

Looking at industry as an organisational system, we can see that productive solidarity means new organisational forms. The links between firms and agents are not fortuitous; they are limited to buying and selling. With production flexibility, third-party schemes in all manufacturing phases have become the norm. Third-party schemes involve mutual agreements of collaboration with shared responsibilities.

Given the increasing influence of demand on the manufacturing process and companies' marketing strategies, the distribution link becomes a critical element in the competition. Distribution means not only retail and wholesale, but also all services related to production such as marketing, advertising, customer service, etc. The importance of advertising in food, drink and tobacco sales cannot be underestimated. These producers are the biggest advertisers in Europe, the United States and Third World countries such as Brazil. Connor et al (1985) estimates that in the 1980s the US consumer paid 10% more, on average, for companies' brand-name products just to cover the publicity cost.

It is in distribution that companies could employ, with advantage, the gains provided by new competitive circumstances. Food retailing, for instance, is linked directly to the consumer. Retailing has excellent conditions in which to assess consumer preferences and so change supply conditions when necessary in order to be competitive.

New information technology such as scanners and bar codes have given supermarkets the opportunity to evaluate their positions every day, using this information to take decisions. Nowadays, in developed countries, supermarkets can obtain sociodemographic profiles of their customers, enabling them to estimate their purchasing habits precisely. Decisions are then taken regarding suppliers, ticket prices, margins and promotions. Food retailing has recently reached a remarkable synergistic stage. On one side consumers provide more information on their preferences and, on the other, the retailer puts on sale exactly what the consumer wants.

As a result of these supermarket advances, consumers increase their identification with point-of-sale and consequently with different retail brands. Supermarkets' possibilities of penetrating the market through their private branded products are growing quickly. In the United Kingdom, where this process is more advanced, retailers have managed to sell private brands to almost every consumer group.[38]

Given the simple technology involved in the manufacture of major foods, beverages and even tobacco, the production of these items is spread among many companies. Innovations are rare: most frequently, traditional products are simply subjected to new forms of presentation. Nowadays, any firm in the food business is able to reproduce, to the same quality, the majority of products made. In reality, what distinguishes one product from another is only the brand name. Not surprisingly, huge amounts are spent by companies for advertising and sales promotion to fix their brands in the consumer's mind. As Rama (1992b) demonstrates, the profits appropriation period is very short in the food industry. Most profits can be obtained immediately after the launch of a new product or a modified old product. Because of this peculiarity, the profit margins are high and remain high until new companies penetrate the market.

In this respect, food distributors have an advantage. Through integration schemes with producers, large supermarket chains can sell their own brands that are of the same quality as top brandname products, but at cheaper prices. Retailers are linked to their industry suppliers and are able to replenish empty shelves within a few hours.

Statistics show a close relationship between supermarket concentration and the distribution of private brands. In most high- and medium–income countries, the ten largest supermarket chains control at least 50% of grocery sales. In these countries the own-brand process has progressed rapidly.

This link between supermarket concentration and private brands, however, may not be valid for all countries. In Brazil, for instance, there is very high supermarket concentration – in the late 1980s, the ten largest supermarket chains held 79% of sales – yet a private brands strategy is almost non-existent (Rama, 1992a; Marion, 1985 and Green, 1992b). On the one hand, this fact demonstrates that the power of industrial supplier companies is still very strong in countries like Brazil. On the other hand, it shows that both supermarkets and small- to medium-sized producers have not achieved any sort of integration in terms of supply.[39]

Given the large amount of inexpensive goods traded in supermarkets within a short time, the managing of logistic systems are critical. In France, investment in business information for retailing activities reached US$4 billion in 1991.[40] That is why a new profitable business is emerging in developed countries: logistic services. According to Green (1992b, p. 53) this is one of the fastest growing businesses in France. In 1986, for instance, 31% of added value – 15.5% of final consumer prices – in the French food industry was held by logistic activities. According to these figures, in areas such as frozen foods the logistic costs can reach 40% of retail sales turnover.

All these elements combine to show that, in the early 1980s, the agro-food system entered into a new phase penetrated by post-fordist techniques. The next section investigates the impact of these changes on Brazil.

Brazil: Crisis and Restructuring

In the last decade Brazil has experienced an intense process of mergers and acquisitions in its food industry. Does this activity mean that Brazil's food industry is undergoing a wide restructuring, or are the examples – as shown in Table II – merely sporadic cases dictated by transitory financial conditions?

For a long time Brazil has been seen as a land of opportunities. Particularly in the case of the food industry, Brazil has been considered a promising investment field due to its alleged comparative advantage. An emerging consumer market, vast sources of raw materials, and cheap labour contributed to this view. Nevertheless, after all the changes in the fordist paradigm regarding production and consumption, what are the future prospects for Brazil?

In terms of Brazil's market advantages, consider the following points:

i) In the last ten years, Brazil has stagnated in terms of growth. *Per capita* income has declined and poverty has increased. Even in this depressed context, however, the food industry grew at a rate slightly higher than population growth and consequently higher than the GNP *per capita* growth. The population grew 2.48% per year in the 1970s dropping to 1.96% per year in the 1980s. Table III compares income growth with the performance of food and beverage sectors in Brazil in recent years.

One may observe that the growth of the food and beverages industries has surpassed the growth of GNP overall. The increase of these sectors in 1980-91 were 27.3% and 30.5%, respectively, compared to 25.1% for GNP and 23.8% for population. Moreover, particularly in the case of the food industry, performance is conducted in a counter-cyclical way with a one year lag. When the economy declines, the food sector decreases less than the whole economy. Alternatively, when the economy goes up this sector also increases relatively less. The common explanation for this phenomenon is the relative non-compressibility of food demand. Even with decreasing income, people have to feed themselves.

Official statistics collected in the last national research study of households show that, in spite of high income concentration and social differences, the Brazilian market has impressive dimensions. Families earning yearly more than ten minimum salaries – approximately US$9,600 per year – represent only 18.2% of Brazilian households, yet these families hold almost 60% of the disposable national income, nearly US$180 billion. Given that, in this income segment, families spend 25% of their income on food, both at home and outside the home, even considering only the richest strata a market of US$45 billion is created.

Table III
Brazil: GNP, GNP *per capita* and Food and Beverages Output Growth (1980-92)

	GNP	GNP *per capita*	Food	Beverages
1980	9.2	6.8	8.0	7.0
1981	-4.5	-6.3	2.7	-7.4
1982	0.5	-1.4	0.9	0.9
1983	-3.5	-5.3	3.3	-5.0
1984	5.3	3.3	-0.7	-0.6
1985	7.9	5.9	0.2	11.0
1986	7.6	5.6	0.3	23.2
1987	3.6	1.6	4.9	-3.4
1988	-0.1	-2.1	-2.4	2.4
1989	3.3	1.2	1.3	14.7
1990	-3.9	-5.9	2.3	-1.3
1991	0.8	-1.1	4.9	1.5
1992	-0.1	-3.0	n.a.	n.a.

Sources: FIBGE and Banco Central do Brasil - Boletim Mensal (various editions)

The highest income strata in Brazil dwell in urban areas, chiefly in the centre-south. This region holds 59.3% of the Brazilian household income. Here, one can see that the Brazilian market is concentrated in two ways: among families and among regions. For the food industry this is a satisfactory operational framework. In this environment, more value added products can be distributed to demand in a concentrated area. Moreover, given the consumer's urban and cosmopolitan profile, the openings created by new shopping and consumer habits are much more advantageous.

ii) Access to sources of raw materials has been widened by the food industry in two ways: first, by the opening and widening of international agricultural trade, and secondly, by the inclusion of substitutes and alternatives to primary raw materials.

Regarding agricultural trade, this is so far a sluggish trend. Most agricultural trade is performed inside commercial blocs. Europe is self-sufficient in most agricultural products. The United States has not only reached self-sufficiency, but also consolidated its position as the largest agricultural exporter in the world in the last decade. The only member of the OECD (Organisation for Economic Cooperation and Development) that remains heavily dependent on agricultural imports is Japan, where the food self-sufficiency is very low at nearly 40% (ABAG 1993, p. 43).[41] For this reason, Japanese investment abroad in the food industry is high and has been concentrated basically in developing countries (Rama, 1992a).

Curiously, the most visible trend in this area, is the recent entry of traditional traders into food production in developed countries. Because of the low profits obtained in international trade, many international companies are opening processing plants in Europe and Asian countries. Contrary to common sense, there is no defining trend within transnational investments. On the one hand, investment flows towards new fields, looking for diversification in developing countries; on the other hand, there is also some investment in complementary areas of food production.

In the case of food products, it appears that since colonial times few things have changed. Developing countries are of interest only in terms of exporting irreplaceable tropical products. This is the main purpose for establishing factories near the sources of raw materials. However, because of protectionism by the wealthy – illustrated by quotas and preferential imports for former colonies – market expansion for these products is difficult and uncertain.

In global terms, proximity to sources of raw materials is not necessarily a competitive advantage in terms of investment. This concept was related to geopolitical issues in the post-war environment, a period when shortages of food and raw materials were seen as a constraint on companies' growth.

Regarding innovations within the agro-food system, however, the introduction of substitutes to natural products is only embryonic. Very few products or ingredients produced in a laboratory enter the market. Despite progresses in biotechnology and genetic engineering, it is too soon to announce a new agricultural or agroindustrial revolution based on these techniques. In fact, in schumpeterian terms, no change in the technological paradigm suggests new products or processes, or even cost reductions, in goods or services for the next decade (see Brown and Goldin, 1992).

There is an exaggerated optimism about the new technologies which suggests that they can create new products to substitute imports. Such products, if produced at competitive costs, could invalidate any natural advantages in the production of raw materials. In other words, natural products could be reproduced at convenience according to different market needs. In this scenario, countries like Brazil would lose their place in raw materials production and in food supply to developed countries. Any discussion of biotechnology's future is misplaced here, however. It is enough to point out that the gains provided by new biotechnology have not shifted the original production framework.

It is important to distinguish between the traditional biotechnologies such as brewing and enzymatic processes and new biotechnologies based on genetic manipulation, tissue breeding and others. Brewing and enzymatic digestion have long been established in the food industry. New biotechnology processes, however, have added only a few products, contributing little to food producers' expertise. Nevertheless, the food industry is one of the sectors in which the new technologies are developing faster.[42]

The radical change that is likely to take place is related to animal and vegetable genetics. New genetically engineered plants such as potato, cotton, tomato, tobacco and soya have already been tested in laboratories and might be introduced to the market very soon, given their better resistance to insects, viruses and even weeds. In the animal sector, efforts to obtain more disease-resistant cattle specimens could be a reality in the short run, as could the introduction of the first genetically manipulated fish. Nevertheless, there is a great uncertainty related to market acceptance of these products; consumer reaction is likely to be negative. Also, the question of intellectual rights on these new products is still controversial (OECD, 1992; Goodman and Redclift, 1991; Wilkinson, 1992).

iii) The cost of Brazilian labour is an important positive factor in terms of comparative advantage. Despite the low quality of the labour force, reduced wages and the absence of industrial action have long been a key element in attracting long term foreign investment capital.[43]

Contrary to common sense, the food, beverage and tobacco industries could be classified among those which have the highest capital intensity. According to Rama, in the United States labour represents only 12% of total industrial costs, half the industrial sector average (1992b, p. 38). Nowadays, most of the processes used by the food industry require little manual work. Given the sophistication of industrial procedures and the spillover of corporate strategies searching for superior market niches, factors such as low-cost labour have lost their former importance. In this new competitive phase, mass production with low costs in a fordist strategy gives way to quality and flexibility. In this new paradigm for the food industry, Brazil is in the early stage of transformation.

Low wages keep out of the market an important part of the Brazilian population. This is another important labour-related aspect that does not fit even within the former fordist pattern. Mass consumption in Brazil is still restricted to parts of the population. Brazil is one of the biggest producers of soya beans, poultry and canned beef. Nevertheless, 'low wages and regressive income distribution weaken the articulation between the production complex of animal grains and mass consumption' (Goodman and Redclift, 1991, p. 164). More than 75% of soya beans are exported, causing integration to a fordist consumption pattern in other countries with little internal integration. In this sense Goodman and Redclift (1991) regard Brazil, as well as Mexico, as a 'proto-fordist' agro-food system.

Since the constitution of a common market, European countries have been doing their best to balance the power of purchase of their food consumers. Green and Rocha dos Santos (1992b) remarked that in Latin America, as a market, the opposite occurred. There are no regulations common to all countries, and transnational companies are not able to operate easily in such a heterogeneous market. Add to this the differences in legislation and consumption patterns as well as infrastructural deficiencies and political instability and it becomes clear why international companies prefer to act in other markets.

Conclusions

The aim of this paper has been to discuss the main aspects of the restructuring of the worldwide food industry and its effects on Brazil. The food industry was one of the first industrial activities to be constituted in Brazil in the last century. Its development until the 1930s was noteworthy for the import substitution process geared to the increasingly urban population. The origin of this first development phase has been identified with the links between the hegemonic agrarian and mercantile capital. At this time, most of the equipment and machinery involved in manufacturing were imported, and so linkages within the sectors of industry were weak.

From the 1920s, the food industry grew and became an important target of foreign investment. Brazil's natural advantages and its huge emerging market have attracted an entire cluster of light industries. In the 1950s, with the establishment of industries in capital and intermediate goods, and with agricultural modernisation, modern food production began in Brazil.

Contributing to this progress was the spread of a consumption pattern similar to that in developed countries, with the so-called fordist diet as support. Among many elements of this second phase of Brazil's food industry were mass production, the growing number of women engaged in the labour market, the introduction of home appliances and new consumer habits.

Despite the large numbers of urban consumers incorporated into the market, the fordist strategy has not taken hold in Brazil. Unlike in other countries in which non-durable production was the basis of subsequent industrialisation, in Brazil this process remained inconclusive. The official policy depressing salaries and the uneven income distribution obstructed the permanent expansion of the market. At the same time, a spurious competitiveness was established emphasised by the high levels of external protection.

From the 1950s industrial policy had shifted towards production of durable goods, leaving non-durables as a non-priority investment area. Economic plans at that time touched only marginally on non-durable goods as a particular target for government incentives. Without taking firm root, food production continued to expand, in absolute terms, towards medium- and upper-class consumers or, alternatively, towards foreign markets.

The mid-1980s saw many changes in ownership positions in the food industry. New sources of capital emerged, mergers took place and new forms of relationship between companies and their market developed in Brazil. Given the restructuring process in the food industry, in this activity is Brazil only reflecting changes in developing countries or do they represent an initial step for a new industrial phase?

Such activity in developed countries is very different in terms of quality from that which took place in Brazil in recent decades. The food industry in developed countries is gradually abandoning the fordist consumer pattern to adapt to a new reality. The dynamic element that drives this new phase is on the demand side, mostly in the food distribution link.

The market power of the big food retailing chains is being used in Europe and the USA to shape and reinforce new consumer habits. Facing a saturated and non-permeable market, retailers and industry have succeeded in segmenting consumer preferences. Recent profit margins for industry and retailers are very impressive. Having failed to widen the consumer base with price reductions, companies instead tried to deepen the consumer base. To this end, remarkable innovations – technical and organisational – have been made to establish a so-called network economy.

The Brazilian market is affected in negative and positive ways by restructuring of the worldwide food industry. There are significant temporal factors such as economic instability and low external opening that hamper the attraction of new foreign capital to Brazil's food sector. Nevertheless, the same transitory circumstances seem to have encouraged the acquisition of new assets in Brazil. Low acquisition prices and an economically depressed framework are attracting many investors to the food sector. In addition, Brazil's relaxed fiscal, environmental and health legislation are favourable factors for new entries into this sector.

Nowadays, new foreign investors and new national companies entering the field are benefiting from joint venture schemes or cooperation agreements in the food sector. These are still only a small part of the observed search for greater efficiency in production and distribution. Brazil is a long way from reaching a new post-fordist production paradigm. Given the observed trends, however, it is clearly heading in that direction.

Notes

1. These activities were established on a new basis and could not be considered enlargements of the so-called Rural Complex.

2. See, for example, Cano (1977), Cardoso de Mello (1975), Dean (1969), Suzigan (1986) and Silva (1976) among others. Note that this subject is quite polemical and has been the subject of a long debate in the Brazilian economic literature.

3. 'Os próprios fazendeiros investiam seus lucros em indústrias diretamente e indiretamente quando seus lucros transitavam pelo sistema bancário (ou eram investidos na própria constituição dos bancos) ou por outra forma qualquer de intermediação financeira e de capital' (Cano, 1977, p. 129).

4. Paim quotes Rangel due to his importance as an exponent of the Rural Complex concept in the agrarian Brazilian literature based on Lenin (*The development of Capitalism in Russia*). In his classic book *A Questão Agrária Brasileira* (Recife: CDEP, 1962), published only years after Gilberto Paim's *Industrialização e Economia Natural*, Rangel applies this concept to a specific situation showing the self-containment of the Brazilian rural economy:

'The peasants, in spite of their ordinary ignorance (sic), are continuously comparing their work in the rural activity, secondary and tertiary activities with other activities placed outside the Rural Complex' (1962, p. 32).

5. In order to demonstrate the lack of monetary relationships in the whole Brazilian economy at that time, Paim notes that the first cloth factory was established in São Paulo only in 1873. Before this many urban factories had

been forced to close down as there were insufficient consumers to sell to. Even the few factories that survived in that period had a difficult time competing with imports.

6. '(...) passava a ser melhor negócio para o fazendeiro desviar escravos das inumeráveis oficinas existentes na grande propriedade para as atividades da lavoura, habituando-se paulatinamente a comprar na cidade, a preço mais baixo, os produtos que antes saiam destas oficinas' (Paim, 1957, p. 46).

7. In addition to cotton mills, sugar mills and sugar refineries, foundries, gun powder factories, breweries and other industrial activities were integrated to the Rural Complex.

8. In those periods the government appealed to a devaluation policy seeking stability in coffee income. Under this policy, all imported goods became expensive with the exception of capital goods, which had received incentives (see Furtado, 1977, p. 197).

9. Until 1930 foreign capital was concentrated in the public services. The only foreign investment of any note in agro-industry occurred in the second half of the 1920s, in the slaughter and cottonseed oil industries. For more on this issue, see Prado Jr. (1970), especially chapter 25.

10. Burbach and Flynn (1982) identify in this period the great industrialisation boom in Latin America that involved huge transfers of capital from transnational companies. In the case of the food industry, the authors mention that one of the causes of this inflow towards industry was the weak performance of agricultural commodities in the international market.

11. The Argentine example is remarkable. The food industry in Argentina was established in the last decades of the nineteenth century. The enlargement of this process was achieved by incorporating gradually new activities that emphasised so-called 'desarrollo hacia dentro'. One can see clearly in the figures how national production substituted step-by-step for imports (see Gatto and Gutman, 1990).

12. '(No Brasil) era praticamente impossível que o processo de industrialização se desse da base para o vértice da pirâmide produtiva, isto é, partindo-se dos bens de consumo menos elaborados e progredindo lentamente até atingir os bens de capital' (Tavares, 1977, p. 46).

13. In the automobile industry, the arrival of European companies such as Mercedes-Benz, DKW, Volkswagen, Renault, Scania and others supplanted US investment. However, in the food sector the US companies already had a vast experience in canned foods with distribution schemes that gave them an

advantage over European companies. Moreover, in the post-war period the food industry in Europe was not doing well.

Figures presented by Baer (1985) for the beginning of the 1950s prove the supremacy of US capital in Brazil. US investments were 43.9% of the total followed by Canada (30.3%), United Kingdom (12.1%), France (3.3%), Uruguay (3.1%), Panama (2.3%) and others (5.0%). For the late 1960s, when the Central Bank began to put together regular statistics on foreign investments in Brazil, the percentages were the following: USA (47.7%), Switzerland (13.9%), Germany (10.4%), Canada (9.8%), United Kingdom (6.4%), Japan (3.2%), France (2.0%) and others (6.6%).

14. Only the first processing from agricultural raw materials is considered here. Also, it should be noted that these different economic censuses are not totally compatible.

15. Souza Cruz now belongs to B. A. T. Industries.

16. *Superhiper* magazine, October 1989, p. 47.

17. The importance of the new links between retailers and food industry must be stressed. This relationship goes beyond buying and selling operations. 'The emergence of supermarkets as a new distribution form has meant a radical change not only in infra-structure but also in (the sector) relationship with other economic sectors. This altered the interdepartmental relationship opening new alternatives to capital circulation, industrial as well commercial' (Fundação Getúlio Vargas, 1980, p. 78).

18. A good summary of the changes occurring in this sector can be found in Muller (1980). The author remarks that in the mid-1970s, when Brazil experienced a meat export boom, ironically the three big foreign firms (Swift, Armour and Wilson) were selling off part or all of their assets.

19. For more on the sugar economy of São Paulo in the eighteenth and nineteenth centuries, see the excellent work of Petrone (1968).

20. Estimated to be 20%, according to Cano (1977, p. 67).

21. Residents of São Paulo State.

22. See Belik (1992, p. 45).

23. Many of these new *'usineiros'* were immigrants who began in Brazil as employees in coffee and sugarcane farms and then progressed to owning farms. This seems to be the case with the Ometto family: Pedro Ometto, the head of

the family, began as a supervisor in the Morganti farms and built a sugar empire. The same happened with the Dedini family: Mario Dedini, the Dedini head of the family was not properly an industrialist but a manager in the Morganti workshops. Nevertheless, many sugar families, from early on, had interests in industry, chiefly textiles, where they participated as small shareholders (Ramos, 1983, p. 85).

24. *Usineiros* means sugarmill owners, but when applied to large plantation owners it is considered an offensive term.

25. This included, for example, Da Barra, São Martinho, São João (Araras), Bonfim, Santa Elisa and Santa Adelia – all in São Paulo State.

26. The company – not a cooperative as it is supposed to be – has a turnover of more than US$2 billion, reaching first place in the Brazilian food industry according to the magazine *Exame – Maiores e Melhores*. The figures were obtained from the 1991 accounts.

27. For an overall description of sugarcane in the northeast, see Pinassi (1987) and Lima (1987).

28. See Cano (1977, p. 221) for interesting remarks on the size of industrial establishments. Food industry companies were quite small, in terms of assets, compared to other industries such as textiles, glass, paper, matches and rope.

29. Figures from Banco Central do Brasil – Boletim Mensal.

30. The biggest mergers identified in the late 1980s were the following: RJR Nabisco (USA) incorporated by KKR (USA) in 1989 – US$24.7 billion; Kraft (USA) incorporated by Philip Morris (USA) in 1989 – US$13.1billion; Pillsbury (USA) by Grand Met (UK) in 1988 – US$5.7 billion; Montedison (ITA) by Ferruzzi (ITA) in 1988 – n.a.; Buitoni (ITA) by Nestlé (SWI) in 1988 – FF 7.0 billion; Rowntree (UK) by Nestlé (SWI) – US$4.3 billion; Martell (FRA) by Seagram (CAN) in 1988 – FF5.2 billion, Heublein (USA) by Grand Met (UK) in 1987 – US$1.2 billion; Courage (UK) by Elders IXL (AUSTRALIA) in 1986 – £1.4 billion; Beatrice Foods (USA) by KKR (USA) in 1986 – US$6.2 billion; Cheeseburgh Pond (USA) by Unilever (NL) in 1986 – US$3.1 billion, Distillers (UK) by Guinness (UK) in 1986 – £2.5 billion; Nabisco (USA) by R. J. Reynolds (USA) in 1985 – US$4.9 billion; General Foods (USA) by Philip Morris (USA) in 1985 – US$5.7 billion; Carnation (USA) by Nestlé (SWI) in 1984 – US$2.9 billion; Esmark (USA) by Beatrice Foods (USA) in 1984 – US$2.8 billion; Carlton (AUSTRALIA) by Elders IXL (AUSTRALIA) in 1983 – AUS$1 billion.

For a complete list of mergers and acquisitions in the last decade see Pérez and

Oncuoglu (1990), Rama (1992a) and Green (1993).

31. According to Goodman and Redclift (1991, p. 139) the United States, under the Public Law 480, exported US$22.3 billion in products between 1954 and 1973. This amount represented 20% of the total agriculture exports in this period. Under PL 480 exports included not only cereals but also cotton, soybeans and dairy products.

32. In food trade activity alone, the concentration is substantial. Goodman and Redclift (1991, p. 166), quoting many authors, mention that between 60% and 90% of agricultural international trade is controlled by only fifteen transnational companies. Taking statistics for each commodity, one can see that between three and six companies have the largest share of the market.

33. Connor et al (1985, p. 5) pointed to the fact that, before World War II, agricultural prices and those of processed food goods were aligned. However, between 1947 and 1972, agricultural prices in the USA dropped 15% at the same time as food prices rose 47%.

34. Including expenditure on tobacco and drinks, this proportion goes up to 22% of household income in Britain.

35. According to Dossier, 'Le restauration collective en Europe' published by *Restauration* magazine (no. 267, 7 May 1993), the catering services in Europe served 2.4 billion meals in 1992.

36. The performance of the world's largest agribusinesses in 1980-85 shows a sales growth rate between 5.17% and 13.54%. The growth in the net profits was outstanding reaching 30.45% in sugar and 25.62% in meat although sectors such as oils and fats have suffered heavy losses (-6.92%) [see Rama (1992a)].

37. According to Zúñiga and Gutiérrez (1992), the sales growth in developed countries did not exceed 0.5% p.a. in recent years. Also, reports of A.C. Nielsen, the international research company, show that Latin America has been the fastest-growing region in terms of food consumption. Among 27 researched countries – 3,000 product categories – analysed between 1987 and 1989, Latin America presented an increase of 15.4% in dairy sales for two years, compared to 3.4% in Europe, 2.1% in North America and 4.0% in the Pacific Rim. For sweets and confectionery the rates were 7.4%, 4.4%, 0.8% and 2.6%.

38. Supermarkets in the United Kingdom lead in private brand sales. On average, UK supermarkets control 30% of groceries sales with private brands. The presence of private brands in other European supermarkets is around 20%. This British leadership can be explained in terms of sales concentration figures. In Britain the top five retailers have more than 60% of grocery sales, making

it one of the most concentrated markets in the world. It is not, however, possible to establish a positive correlation between market concentration and private brand penetration (data obtained from the *Financial Times*, 15 June 1993).

39. US supermarkets are an interesting case. There, the concentration is not as high as in Europe. The ten largest supermarkets have less than 40% of sales, and the penetration of private brands reached only 9% of total sales recently (see *Financial Times* 15 June 1993 and Marion, 1985).

40. According to Green (1993) approximately half of bar-coded prepared points-of-sale in France did not exist three years ago.

41. According to statistics of UNCTAD (United Nations Conference on Trade and Development) the participation of primary imports, including fuel, in total imports was 30.3% in Japan in 1990. The average for the developed countries was 16.1% in the same year.

42. We may speculate that between now and 2000 A.D. the most substantial advances will happen in traditional and conventional areas as new bacteria are developed to enhance flavour and texture, enzymes, biocatalysis, biotests etc. (OECD, 1992).

43. In spite of the low wages, labour costs in Brazil are not so modest. Low labour productivity and multiple duties make the cost of production very high. Pension and union contributions increase this cost to more than 100% of salaries.

Bibliography

ABAG (1993) *Segurança Alimentar: Uma Abordagem de Agribusiness*. São Paulo: ABAG – Associação Brasileira de Agribusiness.

BAER, Werner (1985) *A industrializacão e o desenvolvimento econômico do Brasil*. Rio de Janeiro: Ed. Fundacão Getúlio Vargas.

BELIK, W. (1992) *Agroindústria Processadora e Política Econômica*. Unpublished PhD dissertation, Universidade de Campinas, SP.

BROWN, M. and GOLDIN, I. (1992) *The Future of Agriculture: Developing Country Implications*. Paris: OECD.

BURBACH, R. and FLYNN, P. (1982) *Agroindústria nas Américas*. Rio de Janeiro: Zahar.

BURNS, J. (1983) 'A Synoptic View of Food Industry', in BURNS, J., McINERNEY, J. and SWINBANK, A. (eds.), *The Food Industry – Economics and Politics*. London: Heinemann.

CANDAL, A. (1969) *Industrialização Brasileira: Diagnóstico e Perspectivas*. Brasília: Ministério do Planejamento e Coordenação Geral.

CANO, W. (1977) *Raízes da Concentração Industrial no Brasil*. São Paulo: T.A. Queiroz.

CARDOSO de MELLO, J. M. (1975) *O Capitalismo Tardio: Contribuição à Revisão Crítica da Formação e Desenvolvimento da Economia Brasileira*. Unpublished PhD disssertation, Universidade de Campinas, SP.

CONNOR, J. M. et al. (1985) *The Food Manufacturing Industries – Structure, Strategies, Performance and Policies*. Lexington. Mass.: Lexington Books.

DEAN, W. (1969) *The Industrialization of São Paulo: 1880-1945*. Austin: University of Texas Press.

FANFANI, R. and MONTRESOR, E. (1991) 'Filière, Multinazionali e Dimensione Spaziale nel Sistema Agro-Alimentare Italiano', *La Questione Agrária*. no. 41. Milan.

FIBGE (Fundação Instituto Brasileiro de Geografia e Estatística) (1990) *Censo Industrial do Brasil 1985*, No. 1. Rio de Janeiro: FIBGE.

FUNDAÇÃO GETÚLIO VARGAS (1980) *Investimento Externo e Tendência Oligopolista no Comércio Interno Brasileiro – Um Diagnóstico Preliminar*. São Paulo: Unpublished internal report.

FURTADO, C. (1977) *Formação Econômica do Brasil*. São Paulo: Cia. Editora Nacional (15th edition).

GATTO, F. and GUTMAN, G. E. (1990) 'El Sector Agroalimentário Argentino', in GUTMAN, G. E. and GATTO, F. (eds.), *Agroindustrias en la Argentina*, Buenos Aires: Cepal, pp. 17-43.

GOODMAN, D. and REDCLIFT, M. (1990) 'The Farm Crisis and the Food System: Some Reflections on the New Agenda', in MARSDEN, T. and LITTLE, J. (eds.), *Political, Social and Economic Perspectives on the International Food System*. Aldershot: Gower, pp. 19-35.

GOODMAN, D. and REDCLIFT, M. (1991) *Refashioning Nature: Food, Ecology and Culture*. London: Routledge.

GREEN, Raúl H. (1992a) 'Estratégias e Câmbios Organizativos de los Grupos Alimentários frente al Mercado Único Europeo', in: RODRIGUEZ ZUÑIGA, Manuel (ed.) (1992) *El Sistema Agroalimentario ante el Mercado Único Europeo*. Madrid: Ministerio de Agricultura, Pesca y Alimentación, Editorial NEREA, pp. 35-58.

GREEN, Raúl H. (1992b) 'A Rigor di Logística', *Agricoop – Mensile della cooperazione agrialimentare*. Bologna, Nov/Dec 1992, no. 10, pp. 26-30.

GREEN, Raúl H. (1993) *Principales Tendencias de la Restructuración del Sistema Alimentario Mundial*. Paris: INRA.

GREEN, Raúl H. and ROCHA dos SANTOS, Roseli (1992a) 'Economía de Red y Reestructuración del Sector Agroalimentario', *Desarrollo Económico*, Vol. 32, no. 126 (Jul/Sep), pp. 199-225.

GREEN, Raúl H. and ROCHA dos SANTOS, Roseli (1992b) *Las Multinacionales Alimentarias y la Evolución del Sistema Agroalimentario Mundial*. Paris: INRA.

ILO/UN (1984) *The Social Effects of Technological Developments in the Food and Drink Industries, Including those Arising from New Production Methods and The Need of Training and Retraining*. Food and Drink Industries Committe. Geneva: ILO/UN.

IMF (INTERNATIONAL MONETARY FUND) (1993), *International Financial Statistics Yearbook*. Washington DC: IMF.

KAGEYAMA, A. et al. (1990) 'O Novo Padrão Agrícola Brasileiro: Do Complexo Rural aos Complexos Agroindustriais', in DELGADO, G. C. et al, *Agricultura e Políticas Públicas Brasileiras*, Brasília: IPEA, pp. 113-221 (série IPEA no. 127).

LIMA, J. P. (1987) *Estado e Agroindústria Canavieira no Nordeste: A Acumulação Administrada*, in *Anais do XV Encontro Nacional da ANPEC*. Salvador: Associação Nacional de Posgradação em Economia (ANPEC).

MARION, B. W. (1985) *The Organization and Performance of the U.S. Food System* (Report NC 117/USDA). Lexington, Mass.: Lexington Books.

MAUNDER, P. (1983) 'Competition Policy in the Food Industry', in BURNS, J., McINERNEY, J. and SWINBANK, A. (eds.), *The Food Industry – Economics and Politics*. London: Heinemann.

MULLER, G. (1980) *Estrutura e Dinâmica do Complexo Agroindustrial Brasileiro*. Unpublished PhD dissertation, Universidade de São Paulo.

MULLER, G. (1981) *O Complexo Industrial Brasileiro*. São Paulo: Fundação Getúlio Vargas (Research Paper no. 13).

NIELSEN AVALIA (1990) 'Mercado internacional e destaca potencial latino americano'. Report Nielsen Serviços de Marketing, São Paulo.

OECD (1992) *Biotechnology, Agriculture and Food*. Paris: OECD.

PADIS, P. C. (1977) 'Agricultura e Subdesenvolvimento', in PADIS, P. C. *América Latina. Cinquenta anos de Industrialização*. São Paulo: Hucitec, pp. 219-241

PAIM, G. (1957) *Industrialização e Economia Natural*. Rio de Janeiro: ISEB-MEC (Textos Brasileiros de Economia No. 1).

PEREZ, R. and ONCUOGLU, S. (1990) 'Les Opérations Structurelles des Grands Groupes Agro-Alimentaires', *Economie et Gestion Agro-Alimentaire* (Paris), no. 17, October, pp. 26-32.

PETRONE, M.T.S. (1968) *A Lavoura Canavieira em São Paulo: Expansão e Declínio (1765-1851)*. São Paulo: Difel.

PINASSI, M. O. (1987) *Do Engenho Central à Agroindústria: O Regime de Fornecimento de Canas*. São Paulo: CEDEC (Cadernos CEDEC No. 27).

PIRES, E. and BIELSCHOWSKI, R. (1978) 'Estrutura Industrial e Progresso Técnico na Produção de Laticínios', in *Dois Estudos sobre Tecnologia de Alimentos*. Brasília: IPEA (Série Monográfica no. 27).

PRADO Jr., C. (1970) *História Econômica do Brasil*. São Paulo: Brasiliense. (12th edition).

RAMA, Ruth (1992a) *Investing in Food*. Paris: OECD.

RAMA, Ruth (1992b) 'Tecnología Endógena, Tecnología Exógena', in RODRIGUEZ ZUÑIGA, M. (ed.). (1992) *El Sistema Agroalimentario ante el Mercado Único Europeo*. Madrid: Ministerio de Agricultura, Pesca y Alimentación, Editorial NEREA, pp. 59-79.

RAMOS, P. (1983) *Um Estudo da Evolução e da Estrutura da Agroindústria Canavieira no Estado de S. Paulo (1930/1982)*. Unpublished MA disssertation, Escola de Administração de Empresas de São Paulo da Fundação Getúlio Vargas.

RANGEL, I. (1962) *A Questão Agrária Brasileira*. Recife: Comissão de Desenvolvimento Econômico de Pernambuco.

RASTOIN, J. L. and ALLAYA, M. C. (1990) 'Les Multinationales de l'Agro-Alimentaire à la Fin des Années 80: l'Imperatif de la Mondialisation', *Economie et Gestion Agro-Alimentaire*, no. 17, October, pp. 21-25.

REISS, G. (1983) 'O Crescimento da Empresa Industrial na Economia Cafeeira, São Paulo', *Revista de Economia Politica*, Vol. 3, No. 2 (1983).

RITSON, C., GOFTON, L. and McKENZIE, J. (1986) *The Food Consumer*. Chichester: John Wiley & Sons.

RODRIGUEZ ZUÑIGA, M. and GUTIERREZ, R. S. (1992) 'La Articulación de las Diferentes Etapas del Sistema Agroalimentario: Situación y Perspectivas', in: RODRIGUEZ ZUÑIGA, M. (ed.), *El Sistema Agroalimentario ante el Mercado Unico Europeo*. Madrid: Ministerio de Agricultura, Pesca y Alimentación, Editorial NEREA. pp. 15-34.

SILVA, S. (1976) *Expansão Cafeeira e Origens da Indústria no Brasil*. São Paulo: Alfa-Omega.

SUZIGAN, W. (1986) *Indústria no Brasil*. São Paulo: Brasiliense.

SZMERECSÁNYI, T. (1986) *O Planejamento da Agroindústria Canavieira no Brasil (1930-1975)*. São Paulo: Hucitec-Unicamp.

TAVARES, M. C. (1977) 'Auge e Declínio do Processo de Substituição de Importações no Brasil', in TAVARES, M. C., *Da Substituição de Importações ao Capitalismo Financeiro*. Rio de Janeiro: Zahar (6th edition).

TAVARES, M. C. (1992) 'Ajuste e Reestruturação nos Países Centrais', *Economia e Sociedade* (Campinas), no. 1, pp. 21-58.

WILKINSON, J. (1992) 'La Biotecnología y el Sistema Agroalimentário: Impactos en la Reorganización de las Fases de Producción y Transformación', in: RODRIGUEZ ZUÑIGA, M. (ed.), *El Sistema Agroalimentario ante el Mercado Único Europeo*. Madrid: Ministerio de Agricultura, Pesca y Alimentación, Editorial NEREA, pp. 81-110.

WILLIAMSON, O. E. (1985) *The Economic Institutions of Capitalism – Firms, Markets, Relational Contracting*. New York: The Free Press.